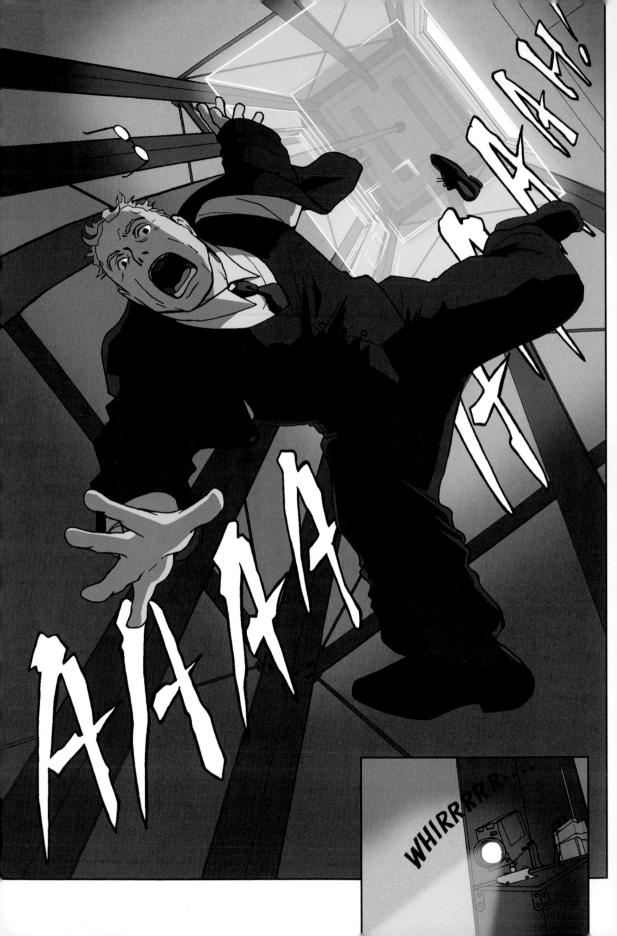

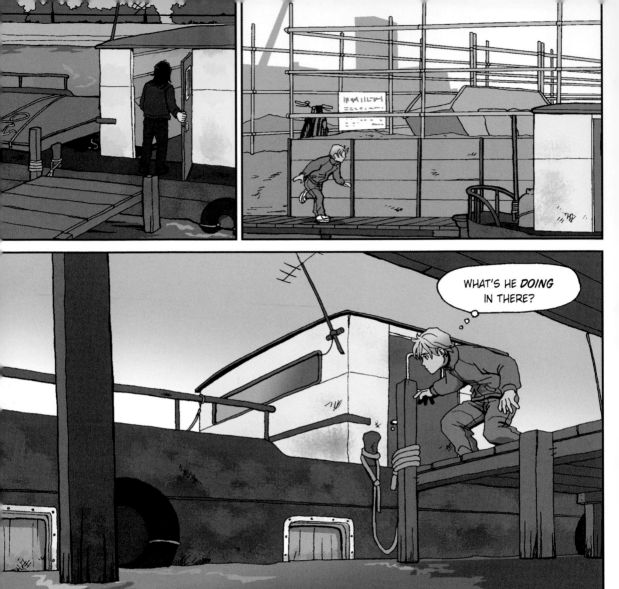

WHAT'S HE *DOING* IN THERE?

HERE GOES NOTHING...

EW.

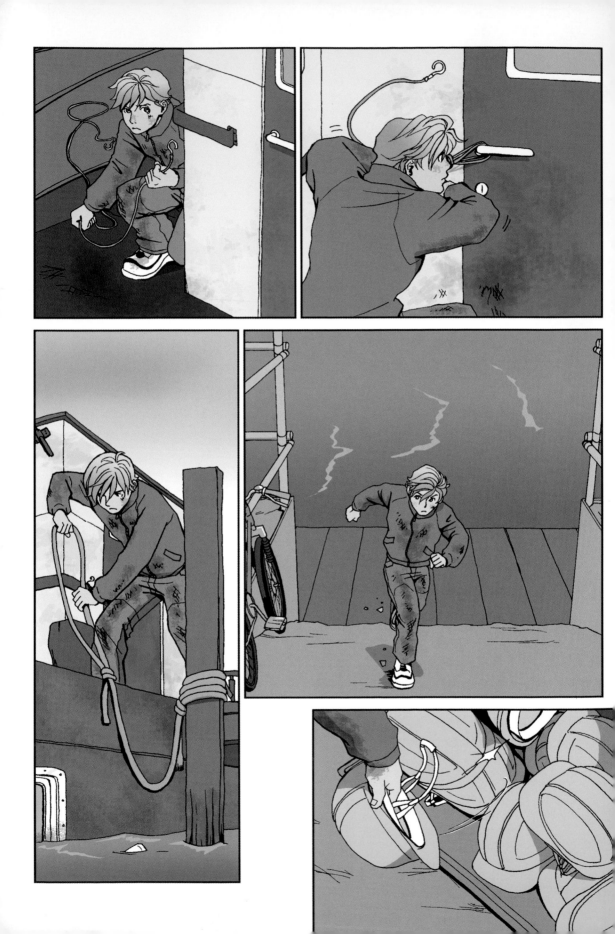

...WE HAVE OVERLOOKED NOTHING! THANKS TO MY PERSONAL INVOLVEMENT AND EFFORTS, WE HAVE NEVER BEEN MORE SUCCESSFUL.
BUT WE ARE NOT RESTING ON OUR LAURELS. OH NO! ANY DAY NOW, WE HOPE TO ANNOUNCE ANOTHER BREAKTHROUGH!
WINNING THE WAR AGAINST DRUGS
KER-RASH
RIVERSIDE CONFERENCE CENTRE

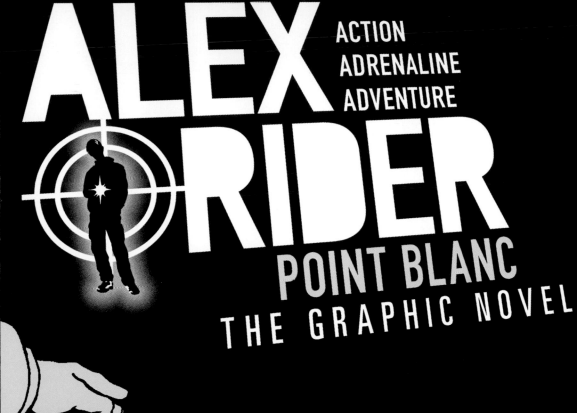

ALEX RIDER

ACTION
ADRENALINE
ADVENTURE

POINT BLANC
THE GRAPHIC NOVEL

ANTHONY HOROWITZ

ANTONY JOHNSTON • KANAKO • YUZURU

WALKER

This is a work of fiction. Names, characters, places and incidents are either the product of the author's imagination or, if real, are used fictitiously. All statements, activities, stunts, descriptions, information and material of any other kind contained herein are included for entertainment purposes only and should not be relied on for accuracy or replicated as they may result in injury.

First published 2007 by Walker Books Ltd
87 Vauxhall Walk, London SE11 5HJ

This edition published 2016

4 6 8 10 9 7 5 3

Text and illustrations © 2007 Walker Books Ltd
Based on the original novel *Point Blanc* © 2001 Stormbreaker Productions Ltd

Trademarks © 2009 Stormbreaker Productions Ltd
Alex Rider™, Boy with Torch Logo™, AR Logo™

This book has been typeset in Wild Words and Serpentine Bold

Printed in China

All rights reserved

British Library Cataloguing in Publication Data:
a catalogue record for this book is available from the British Library

ISBN 978-1-4063-6633-4

www.walker.co.uk

WELL. I'M VERY **SORRY** ABOUT MR ROSCOE. BUT WHAT'S IT GOT TO DO WITH **ME?**

THE DAY **BEFORE** HE DIED, ROSCOE MADE A PERSONAL CALL TO **THIS** OFFICE, ASKING FOR **MR BLUNT**.

I MET ROSCOE AT **CAMBRIDGE UNIVERSITY**, A LONG TIME AGO. WE BECAME **FRIENDS**.

UNFORTUNATELY, I WASN'T HERE TO **TAKE** THE CALL. I ARRANGED TO SPEAK WITH HIM THE NEXT DAY, BUT BY THEN IT WAS **TOO LATE**.

WHAT DID HE WANT?

AND AN **ONLY CHILD**. HE AND ROSCOE HAD A **DIFFICULT** RELATIONSHIP AFTER MICHAEL **DIVORCED** A FEW YEARS AGO.

I SPOKE TO HIS **ASSISTANT**, AND IT SEEMS MR ROSCOE WAS VERY CONCERNED ABOUT HIS SON, **PAUL**.

PAUL CHOSE TO LIVE WITH HIS FATHER, BUT THEY DIDN'T REALLY GET **ON**.

PAUL IS FOURTEEN.

PAUL WAS DOING BADLY AT **SCHOOL**. HE WAS PLAYING **TRUANT**, HANGING AROUND WITH A **BAD CROWD**, GETTING INTO TROUBLE WITH THE **POLICE**...

I SPOKE TO ROSCOE FROM TIME TO TIME, AND HE **WAS** WORRIED THAT PAUL WAS GETTING OUT OF **CONTROL**. BUT THERE DIDN'T SEEM MUCH HE COULD **DO**.

SO IS THAT WHAT YOU WANT *ME* FOR? TO *MEET* THIS BOY, AND TALK TO HIM ABOUT HIS FATHER'S *DEATH*?

NO.

THIS IS GENERAL *VIKTOR IVANOV*, EX-*KGB*.

UNTIL LAST DECEMBER HE WAS HEAD OF THE *FOREIGN INTELLIGENCE SERVICE* AND THE SECOND MOST *POWERFUL* MAN IN *RUSSIA*, AFTER THE PRESIDENT.

BUT SOMETHING HAPPENED TO *HIM*, TOO.

A BOATING ACCIDENT ON THE *BLACK SEA*. HIS BOAT *EXPLODED*, AND NOBODY KNOWS WHY.

WAS HE A *FRIEND* OF ROSCOE'S?

I DOUBT THEY EVER MET.

BUT OUR COMPUTERS *HAVE* THROWN UP ONE STRANGE COINCIDENCE.

IVANOV *ALSO* HAD A FOURTEEN-YEAR-OLD SON, *DIMITRY*.

AND DIMITRY IVANOV *DEFINITELY* KNEW PAUL ROSCOE ... BECAUSE THEY WENT TO THE *SAME SCHOOL*.

WHAT WAS A *RUSSIAN* BOY DOING AT A SCHOOL IN *NEW YORK*?

THEY WEREN'T *IN* NEW YORK.

DO YOU KNOW WHAT A *FINISHING SCHOOL* IS, ALEX?

ISN'T THAT WHERE *RICH PEOPLE* USED TO SEND THEIR *DAUGHTERS*, TO LEARN *TABLE MANNERS?*

THAT'S RIGHT. BUT THIS SCHOOL IS FOR *BOYS* ONLY, AND NOT JUST *ORDINARY* BOYS.

THE FEES AT *POINT BLANC* ARE *TEN THOUSAND POUNDS* A TERM.

IT'S RIGHT ON THE FRENCH-SWISS BORDER, IN THE *FRENCH ALPS.*

THE NAME LITERALLY MEANS *"WHITE POINT".*

IT'S A *REMARKABLE* PLACE, AS YOU CAN SEE. BUILT AS THE PRIVATE HOME OF SOME *LUNATIC* IN THE NINETEENTH CENTURY.

WHEN HE DIED, IT BECAME AN *ASYLUM.*

THEN THE *GERMANS* TOOK IT OVER IN THE SECOND WORLD WAR, AS A *LEISURE CENTRE* FOR THEIR SENIOR STAFF. AFTER THAT IT FELL INTO *DISREPAIR...*

...UNTIL BOUGHT BY ITS CURRENT OWNER, THE ENIGMATIC *PRINCIPAL* OF POINT BLANC ACADEMY.

DR HUGO GRIEF.

POINT BLANC TAKES IN BOYS WHO HAVE BEEN *EXPELLED* FROM ALL THEIR *OTHER* SCHOOLS.

THERE ARE ONLY EVER SIX OR SEVEN PUPILS AT A TIME.

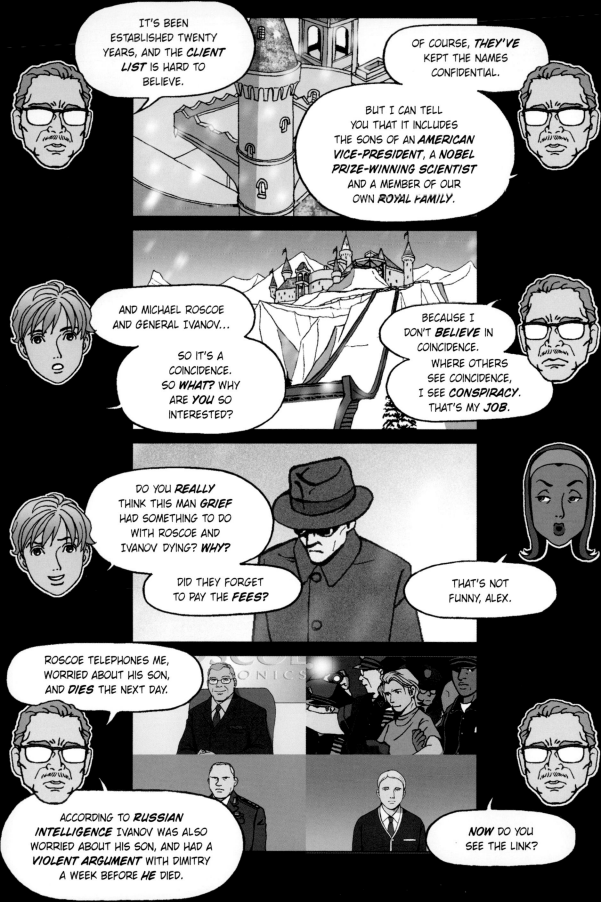

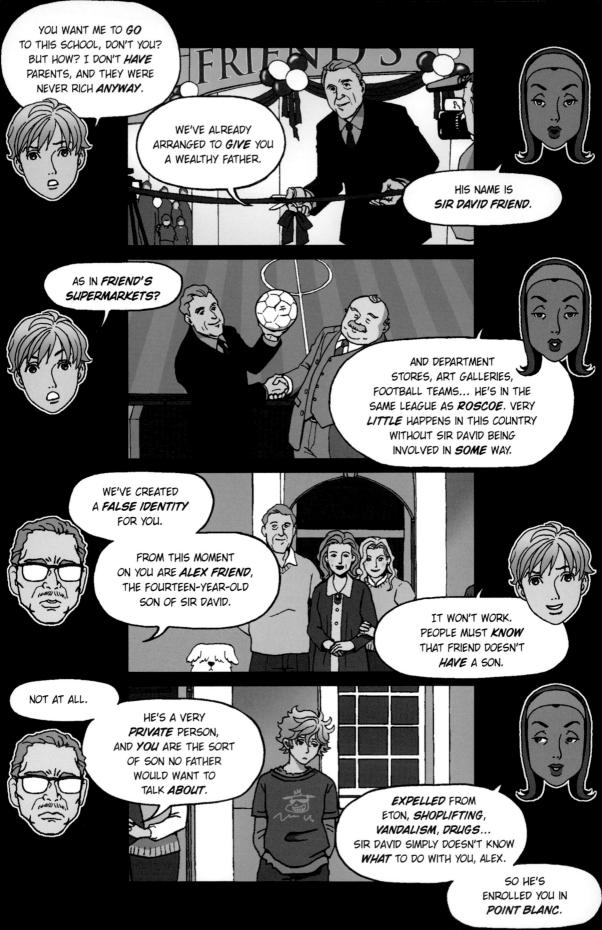

YOU HAVE **ONE WEEK** TO MEMORIZE YOUR **COVER STORY** AND THE FAMILY DETAILS. YOU'LL BE PICKED UP NEXT SATURDAY FROM THE FRIEND'S **COUNTRY ESTATE** IN **LANCASHIRE**.

AND WHAT DO I **DO** WHEN I GET TO THE SCHOOL?

SIMPLY FIND OUT **EVERYTHING** YOU CAN. IT **MAY** BE THAT POINT BLANC IS PERFECTLY **ORDINARY**, AND IN FACT THERE WAS **NO** CONNECTION BETWEEN THESE DEATHS.

IF SO, WE'LL PULL YOU OUT. WE JUST WANT TO BE **SURE**.

SORRY, ALEX.

THEY DON'T ALLOW **GAMES** IN THE SCHOOL. BUT WE'LL **ARRANGE** ALL THAT BEFORE YOU GO, DON'T WORRY.

...

HOW WILL I GET IN **TOUCH** WITH YOU? HAVE YOU MADE ME ANOTHER **NINTENDO**?

IN THE MEANTIME, WE'LL HAVE TO DO **SOMETHING** ABOUT YOUR **APPEARANCE**. YOU DON'T EXACTLY LOOK THE **PART**.

...WHAT?

I HAVE DECIDED TO MOVE THE GEMINI PROJECT INTO ITS LAST PHASE.
POINT BLANC ACADEMY, FRANCE
I UNDERSTAND, DOCTOR.
BUT ARE YOU SURE WE'RE READY?
WITH TWO UNSATISFACTORY RESULTS IN THE LAST FEW MONTHS, WE HAVE NO CHOICE.
BESIDES THE EXPENSE OF ARRANGING THOSE TERMINATIONS, SOMEONE MAY YET CONNECT THE DEATHS OF IVANOV AND ROSCOE ... THOUGH I DOUBT IT.
THE CIA, MI6, EVEN THE KGB ... PAH! THEY'RE SHADOWS OF WHAT THEY USED TO BE.
NEVERTHELESS, THE SOONER WE FINISH THIS PHASE, THE MORE CHANCE OF REMAINING ... UNNOTICED.
WHEN IS THE FINAL BOY ARRIVING?
ALEX FRIEND? I'M PICKING HIM UP FROM ENGLAND TOMORROW.
EXCELLENT. YOU WILL TAKE HIM TO PARIS ON THE WAY HERE?
IF THAT IS YOUR WISH, DOCTOR.
IT IS VERY MUCH MY WISH, MRS STELLENBOSCH. WE CAN DO THE PRELIMINARY WORK THERE. NOW, WHAT ABOUT THE SPRINTZ BOY?

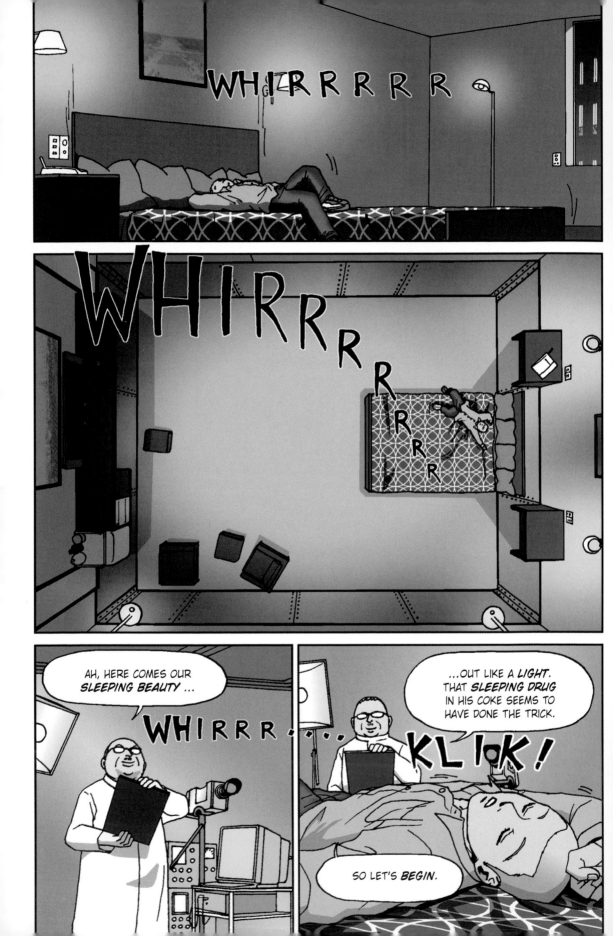

NICE PLACE.

YOU *THINK* SO? THE BUILDING WAS DESIGNED BY A *FRENCHMAN* WHO WAS CERTAINLY THE WORLD'S *WORST* ARCHITECT.

THIS WAS HIS *ONLY* COMMISSION. WHEN THE FIRST OWNERS MOVED IN, THEY HAD HIM *SHOT*.

THERE ARE STILL QUITE A *FEW* PEOPLE HERE WITH *GUNS*.

THAT'S VERY *KIND*, BUT I DON'T REALLY WANT TO *BE* HERE. SO IF YOU'LL JUST TELL ME HOW I CAN GET DOWN INTO *TOWN*, I'LL CATCH THE NEXT TRAIN HOME.

THERE IS *NO* WAY DOWN INTO TOWN. THE SKIING SEASON IS *OVER*, AND THE DESCENT IS NOW TOO *DANGEROUS*.

THERE IS ONLY THE *HELICOPTER* ... AND THAT WILL TAKE YOU FROM HERE ONLY WHEN *I* SAY SO.

ALL THE BOYS HERE COME FROM FAMILIES OF GREAT *WEALTH* AND *IMPORTANCE*, LIKE YOURSELF.

WE COULD VERY EASILY BECOME A TARGET FOR *TERRORISTS*, SO THE GUARDS ARE FOR *YOUR* PROTECTION.

YOU ARE *HERE*, ALEX, BECAUSE YOU HAVE *DISAPPOINTED* YOUR PARENTS.

YOU WERE EXPELLED FROM SCHOOL, YOU HAVE HAD DIFFICULTIES WITH THE *POLICE—*

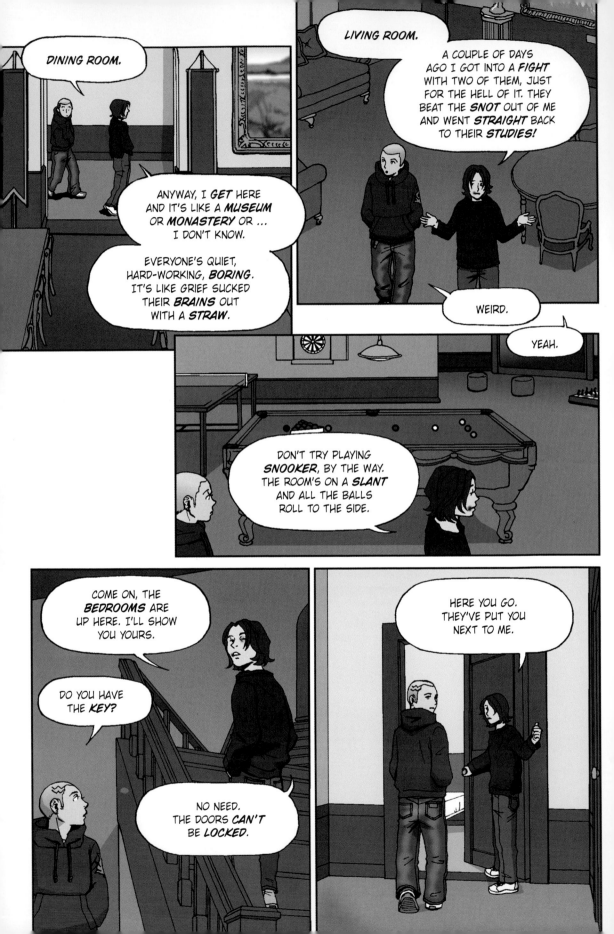

HUGO VRIES (14) Dutch, lives in Amsterdam. Father's name: Rudi, owns diamond mines. Speaks little English. Reads and plays guitar. Very solitary. Sent to PB for shoplifting and arson.

TOM McMORIN (14) Canadian, from Vancouver. Parents divorced. Mother runs media empire (newspapers, TV). Well-built, chess player. Car thefts and drunken driving.

NICOLAS MARC (14) French, from Bordeaux? Expelled from private school in Paris, cause unknown - drinking? Very fit all-rounder. Good at sport but hates losing. Tattoo of devil on left shoulder. Father: Anthony Marc - airlines, pop music, hotels. Never mentions his mother.

CASSIAN JAMES (14) American.
Mother: Jill, studio chief in
Hollywood. Parents divorced.
Loud voice. Swears a lot.
Plays jazz piano. Expelled from
three schools. Various drug
offences - sent to PB after
smuggling arrest but won't talk
about it now. One of the kids
who beat up James. Stronger
than he looks.

JOE CANTERBURY (14) American.
Spends a lot of time with Cassian
(helped him with James).
Mother (name unknown) New York
senator. Father something big at
the Pentagon. Vandalism, truancy,
shoplifting. Sent to PB after
stealing and smashing up car.
Vegetarian. Permanently chewing
gum. Has he given up smoking?

JAMES SPRINTZ (14) German,
lives in Düsseldorf. Father: Dieter
Sprintz, banker, well-known
financier (the One Hundred Million
Dollar Man). Mother living in
England. Expelled for wounding a
teacher with an airpistol. My only
friend at PB! And the only one
who really hates it here.

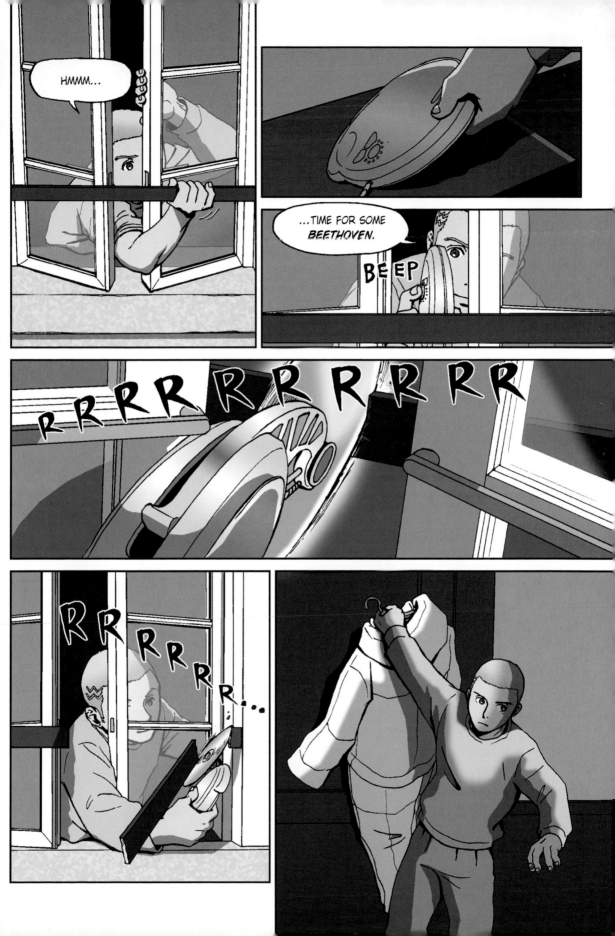

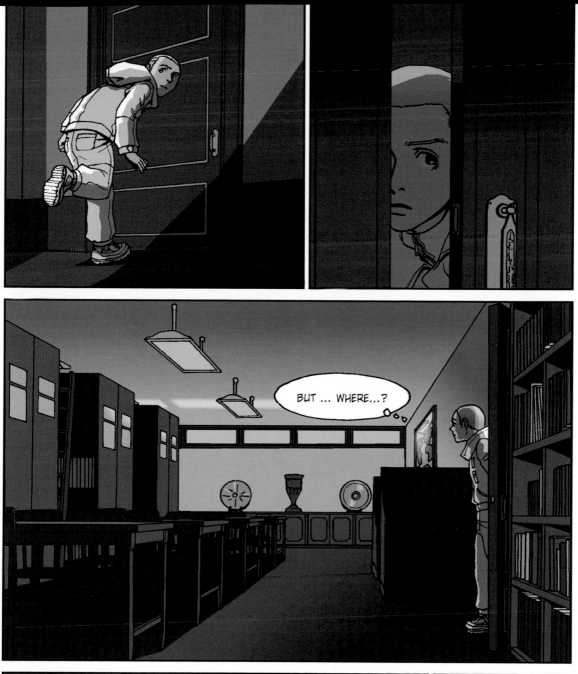

BUT ... WHERE...?

THAT'S THE ONLY DOOR...

...OR *IS* IT?

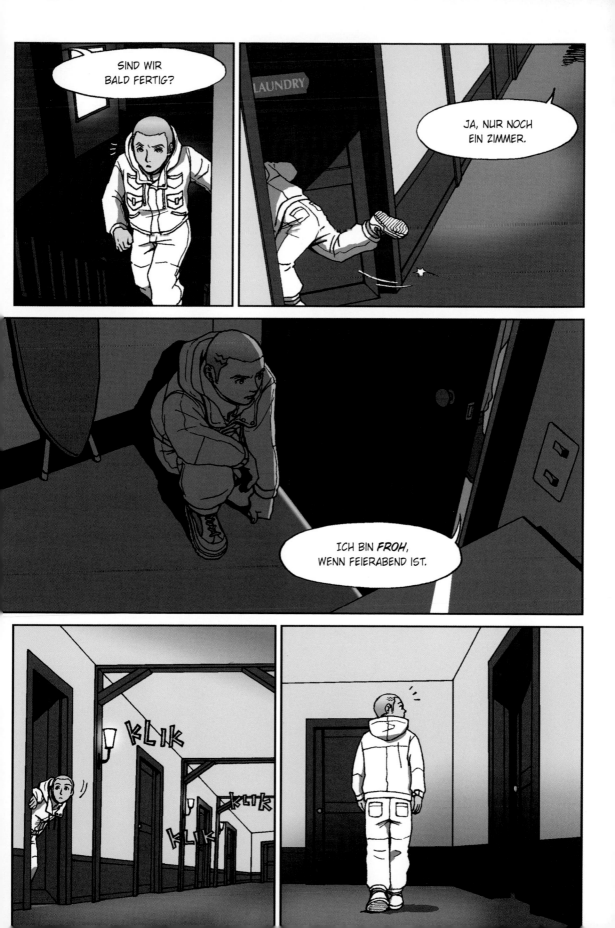

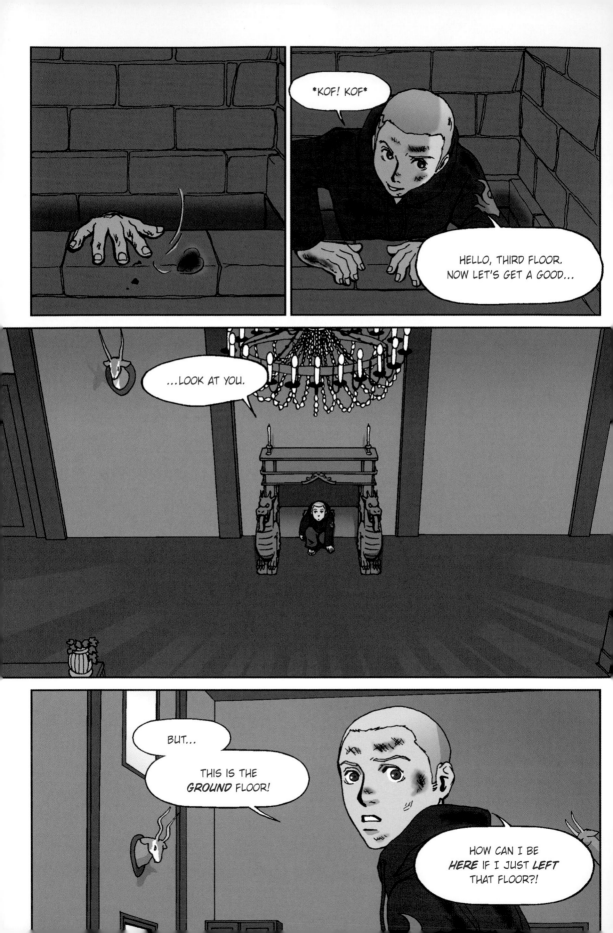

...YOU HAVE **COMPLETED** THE WORK. I AM **GRATEFUL** TO YOU, MR BAXTER.

THANK YOU, DR GRIEF.

SO, I HOPE YOU'RE **PLEASED** WITH THE LAST OPERATION.

ENTIRELY. I SAW HIM AS SOON AS THE **BANDAGES** CAME OFF.

YOU HAVE DONE EXTREMELY WELL.

THIS IS **GRIEF**.

I HAVE SOME **GARBAGE** IN THE OPERATING THEATRE THAT NEEDS TO BE REMOVED. INFORM THE **DISPOSAL TEAM**.

SHHHHHUNK

SHHHHHHUNK

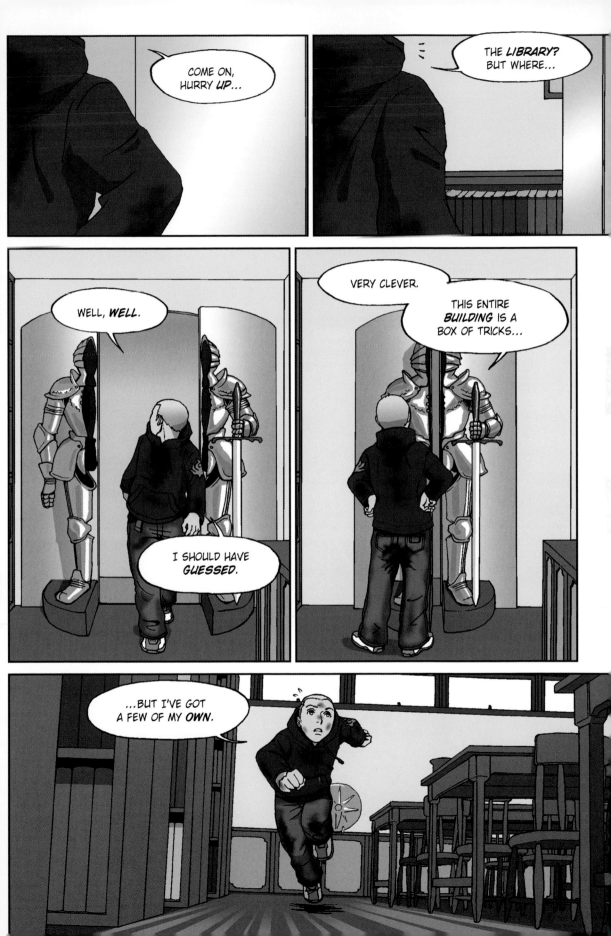

POINT BLANC ACADEMY
24 HOURS LATER

HEY, ALEX! COMING TO *LATIN* THIS MORNING?

LATIN'S A WASTE OF TIME.

IS *THAT* WHAT YOU THINK?

YOU'RE THE ONE WHO'S *WASTING* HIS *TIME*, ALEX.

WHATEVER. YOU ENJOY IT.

HOW **WEAK** AND **PATHETIC** THE WORLD WAS BECOMING ... **DETERMINED** TO GIVE AWAY A **GREAT** COUNTRY LIKE MINE TO PEOPLE WHO HAD **NO IDEA** HOW TO RUN IT.

OH, GREAT. ANOTHER **WANNABE WORLD CONQUEROR**.

OOF!

I LOOKED **AROUND** AND SAW THAT THE PEOPLE OF AMERICA AND EUROPE HAD BECOME **STUPID** AND **WEAK**. THE FALL OF THE **BERLIN WALL** ONLY MADE THINGS WORSE. SOON, EVEN **RUSSIA** WAS INFECTED WITH THE SAME DISEASE.

AND I THOUGHT TO MYSELF, HOW MUCH **STRONGER** THE WORLD WOULD BE IF **I** RULED IT. HOW MUCH **BETTER**.

ON THE **CONTRARY**, IT HAS BEEN THE AMBITION OF VERY **FEW** MEN TO RULE THE ENTIRE WORLD. HITLER, NAPOLEON, STALIN ... GREAT MEN, **REMARKABLE** MEN!

MEN LIKE **ME!**

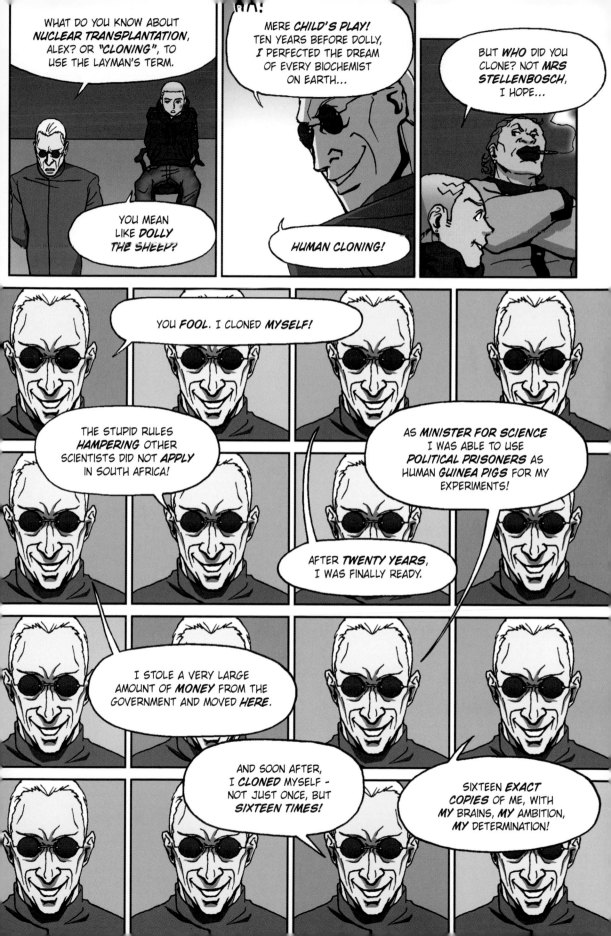

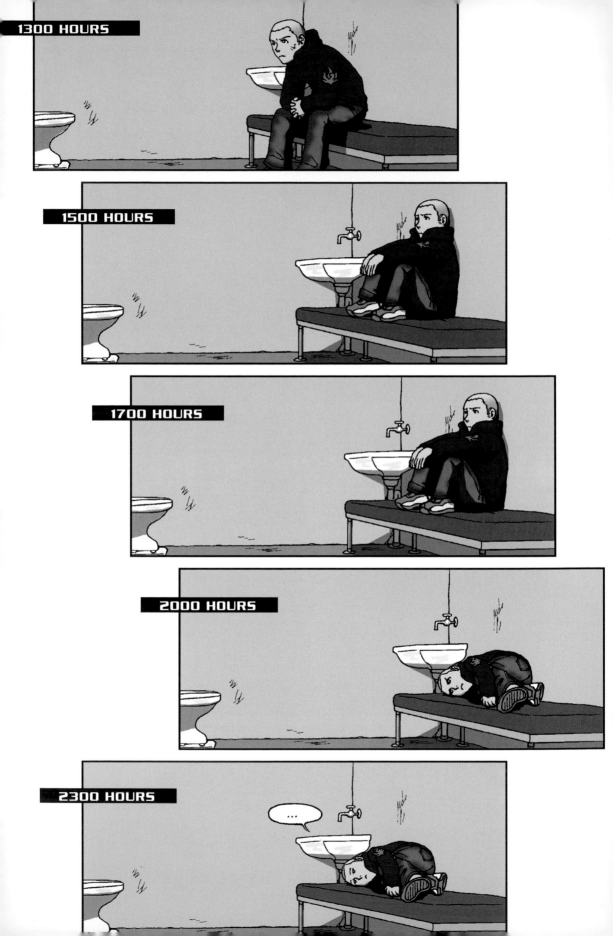

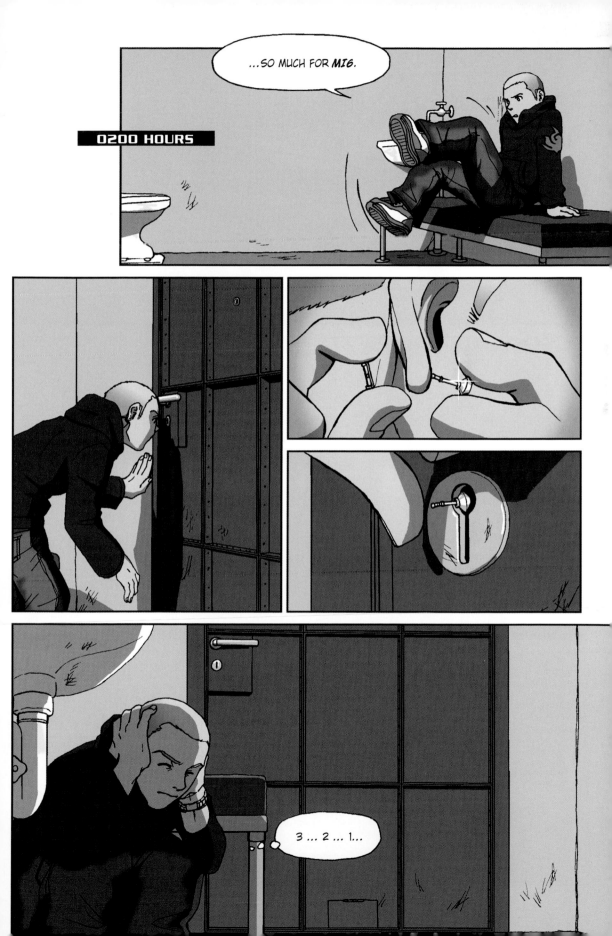

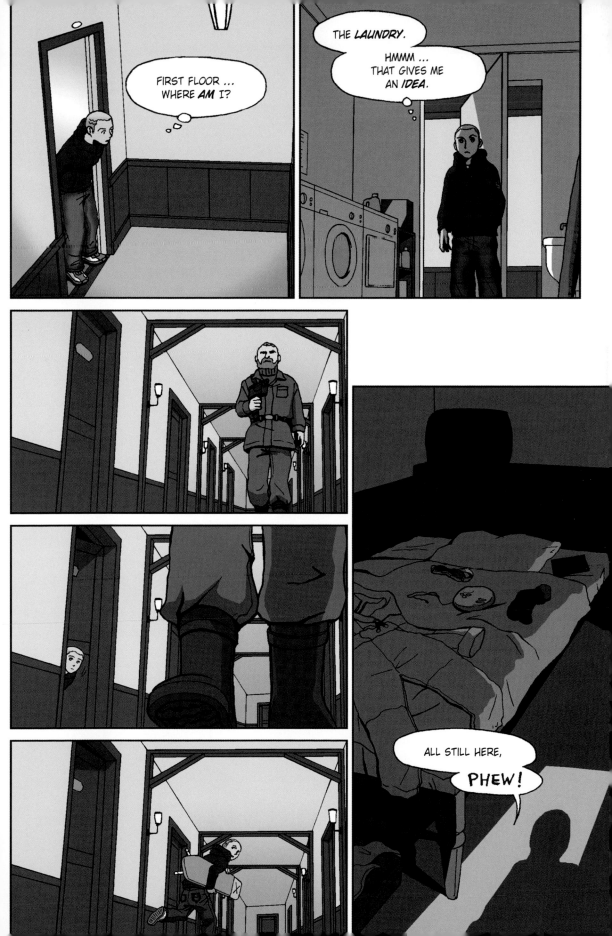

GRENOBLE HOSPITAL
0500 HOURS

FRAU STELLENBOSCH?
ICH HABE *GUTE*
NACHRICHTEN
FÜR SIE...

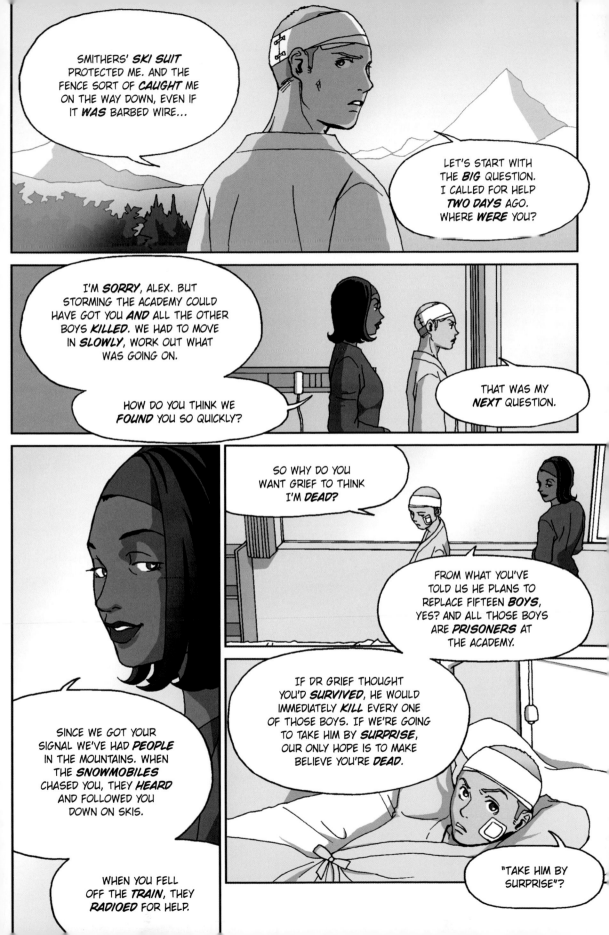

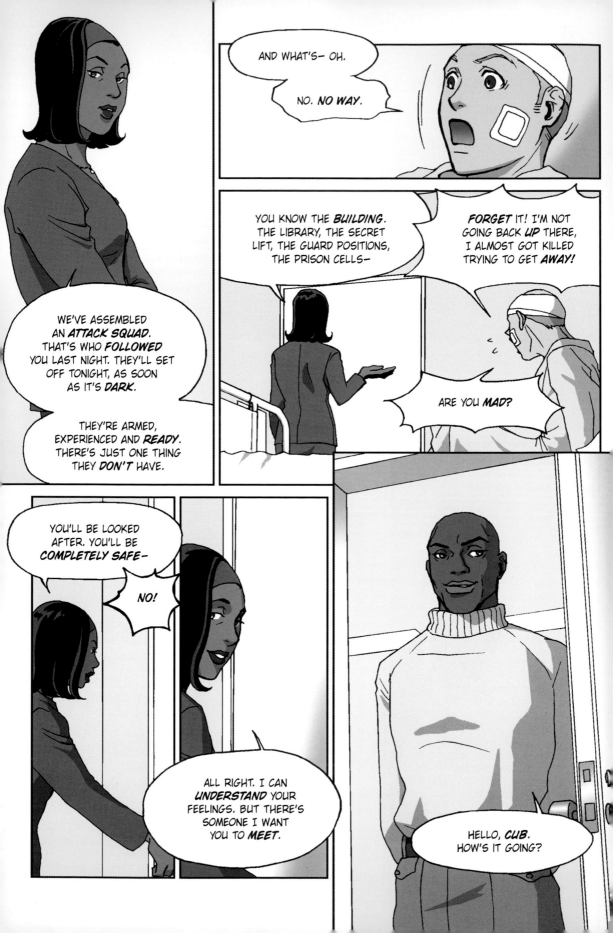

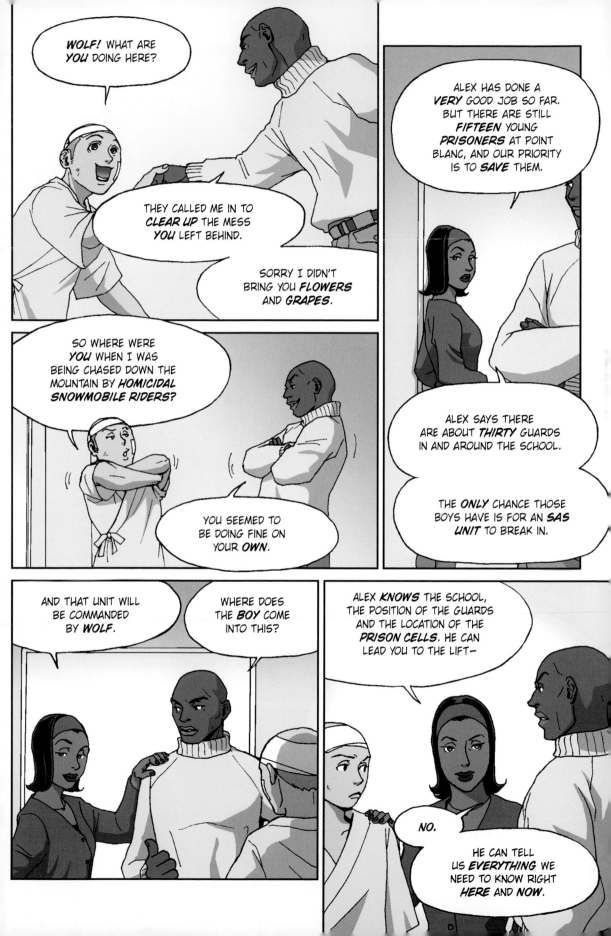

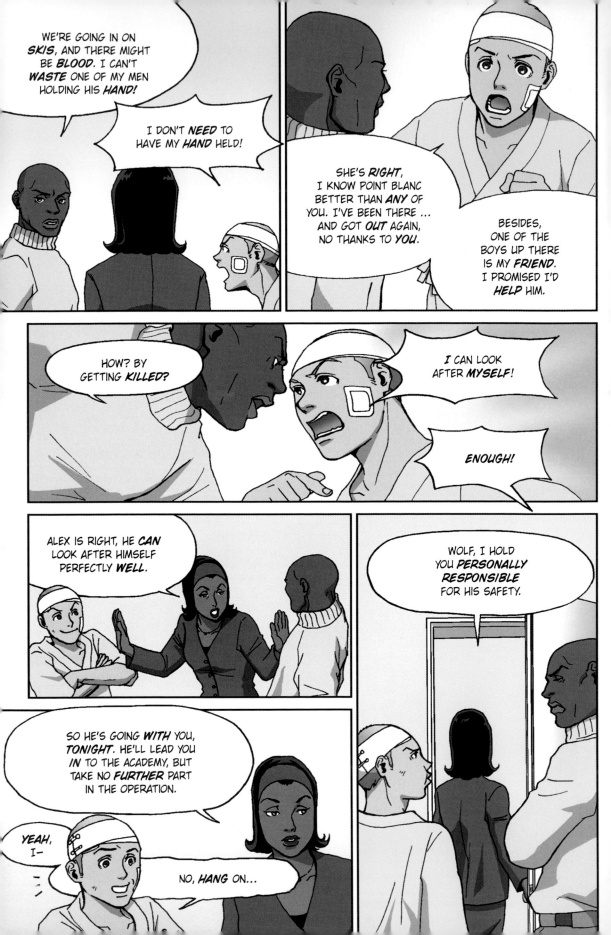

TWO KILOMETRES
NORTH OF POINT BLANC

BROOKLAND SCHOOL

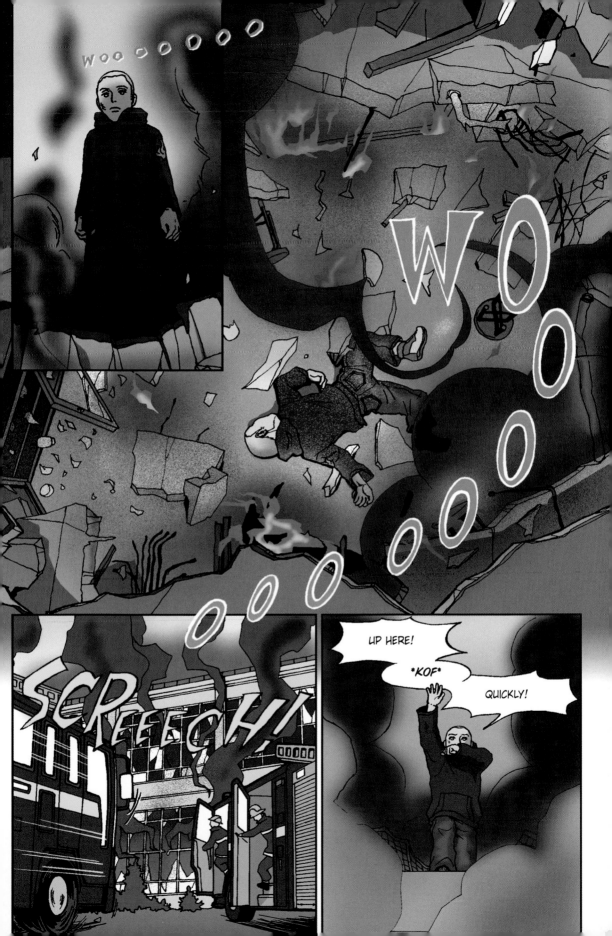

ANTHONY HOROWITZ is the author of the number one bestselling Alex Rider books and The Power of Five series. He has enjoyed huge success as a writer for both children and adults, most recently with the latest adventure in the Alex Rider series, RUSSIAN ROULETTE, and the highly acclaimed Sherlock Holmes novels, THE HOUSE OF SILK and MORIARTY. Anthony was also chosen by the Ian Fleming estate to write the new James Bond novel, TRIGGER MORTIS, which was published in September 2015. Anthony has won numerous awards, including the Bookseller Association/Nielsen Author of the Year Award, the Children's Book of the Year Award at the British Book Awards, and the Red House Children's Book Award. In 2014 Anthony was awarded an OBE for Services to Literature. He has also created and written many major television series, including INJUSTICE, COLLISION and the award-winning FOYLE'S WAR.

www.anthonyhorowitz.com

ANTONY JOHNSTON, who wrote the script for this book, is a veteran author of comics and graphic novels, from superheroes such as DAREDEVIL and WOLVERINE, to science-fiction adventures like WASTELAND and DEAD SPACE, and even thrillers such as THE COLDEST CITY and JULIUS. He also writes videogames, including many of the DEAD SPACE series, and other games like BINARY DOMAIN and XCOM. His debut fiction novel FRIGHTENING CURVES won an IPPY award for Best Horror. Antony lives in North-West England with his partner Marcia, his dogs Connor and Rosie, and far too many gadgets with apples printed on them.

www.antonyjohnston.com

The artwork in this graphic novel is the work of two artists, **KANAKO DAMERUM** and **YUZURU TAKASAKI**, who collaborate on every illustration. Although living on opposite sides of the globe, these Japanese sisters work seamlessly together via the Internet.

Living and working in Tokyo, **YUZURU** produced all the line work for these illustrations using traditional means. The quality of her draughtsmanship comes from years of honing her skills in the highly competitive world of manga.

KANAKO lives and works out of her studio in London. She managed and directed the project as well as colouring and rendering the artwork digitally using her wealth of knowledge in graphic design.

www.manga-media.com
www.thorogood.net

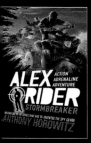

STORMBREAKER

Alex Rider – you're never too young to die…

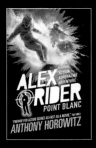

POINT BLANC

High in the Alps, death waits for Alex Rider…

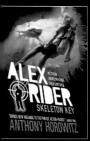

SKELETON KEY

Sharks. Assassins. Nuclear bombs. Alex Rider's in deep water.

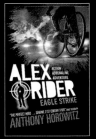

EAGLE STRIKE

Alex Rider has 90 minutes to save the world.

SCORPIA

Once stung, twice as deadly. Alex Rider wants revenge.

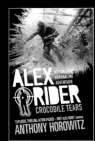

ARK ANGEL

He's back – and this time there are no limits.

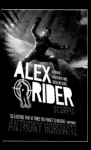

SNAKEHEAD

Alex Rider bites back…

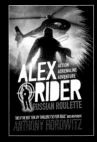

CROCODILE TEARS

Alex Rider – in the jaws of death…

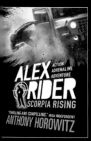

SCORPIA RISING

One bullet. One life. The end starts here.

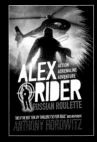

RUSSIAN ROULETTE

Get your hands on the deadly prequel.

alexrider.com